The Legend of Being Irish
A Collection of Irish-American Poetry

Edited by David Lampe

WHITE PINE PRESS

DEDALUS PRESS

ISBN 0-934834-23-7

This book is co-published and distributed in Ireland by Dedalus Press.

This publication was made possible, in part, by grants from the New York State Council on the Arts and the City of Buffalo.

Design by Watershed Design.

Printed in the United States of America.

WHITE PINE PRESS
P.O. Box 236
Buffalo, New York 14201
*
76 Center Street
Fredonia, New York 14063

CONTENTS

Travel/Exile/Return

Celebrations: First Appearance Poems

INTRODUCTION

As far as I know, this is the first anthology of modern Irish-American and American-Irish poetry to be collected. It is thus doubly ironic that the selection should be made by someone who is not Irish (except by interest) and by someone who has even atttacked the idea of anthologies and the fixing of literary canons. Obviously some explanation is necessary.

I grew up in a small Iowa farm community which differed from Garrison Keilor's Lake Woebegone in not having a lake and substituting Swedes for Norwegians. In such a world Irish were exotic both in religion and style. I early heard and treasured the story of how my Swedish grandfather and P.J. Mullen defied the KKK in a local election. Joyce's *Portrait* was an important book for me in high school, and in college I continued to read and enjoy Irish writing. During my senior year I directed a production of Synge's "Riders to the Sea." In graduate school I was lured into the study of Chaucer and the European Middle Ages, a Catholic world view that I still "profess" in the classroom today.

When I came to Buffalo in 1969, I found that because of the amazing collection of Joyce materials in the Lockwood Poetry Room, State University of New York at Buffalo (SUNYAB) was bringing major Joyce scholars for summer session lectures. I took advantage of those opportunities to hear and learn, taught my way through *Ulysses* with the aid of Richard Ellman's fine lectures, and in 1974 met John Montague who was a guest at SUNYAB for the summer. I arranged for him to read at SUNY College at Buffalo. It was a memorable occasion. During his reading of "Cave of Night" from the manuscript of *Slow Dance* a dog in the audience began to bark wildly. James Wright (also in residence that summer) provided us with Goethe's explanation: a dog barks when the Devil appears. Someone else muttered that it was, after all, an Irish Setter. Montague has since returned to Buffalo many times, most recently to receive an honorary degree from SUNY College at Buffalo and to deposit his papers and manuscripts at the SUNYAB Poetry Room. Indeed, the germ of this collection was his suggestion that something interesting was happening in modern Irish-American literature.

A few years later I did the preliminary work for this collection when a colleague asked me to take over his Irish-American history seminar for a couple meetings. It was then I discovered the truth of Montague's suggestion; something interesting was happening in Irish-American poetry of the last 25 years, the period since the election of John F. Kennedy. Irish-American poets were finally, without shame and without shamrocks, writing about their unique experiences as Irish-Americans.

In some cases that still meant casting an eye toward the "old sod," but that glance, as in the case of Alan Dugan or Paul Hogan, could be angry and the resultant poetry caustic or cautionary; no more "Danny Boy."

For many American Irish the journey home to Ireland has only been possible for the third or fourth generations, who, equipped with college educations if not immediate racial memories, had the more and imaginative visions of Yeats, Joyce, O'Casey, and Beckett to sharpen their perceptions of place and tradition. Some, with Patrick Kavanaugh, have been ready to "stuff" rather than excuse the stage Irish cliches; others have glorified in the opportunity and occasion to find themselves amidst the evidences of ancestral achievements and anguish. But finally and fruitfully they have begun to acknowledge that they are Irish and investigate and understand the various legends of being Irish in America.

—"History is a nightmare from which I am trying to awake."

This collection is arranged according to several principles of order. "Irishness," in Conor Cruise O'Brien's classic formulation, "is not primarily a question of birth, or blood, or language; it is the condition of being involved in the Irish situation, and usually of being mauled by it." Hence my selection begins with poems reflecting on Irish history. Marianne Moore invokes "Spenser's Ireland" both to understand "the greenest place I've ever seen" and herself, for she anticipates O'Brien's definition in her famous last lines:

> The Irish say your trouble is their
> trouble and your
>   joy their joy? I wish
> I could believe it;
> I am troubled, I'm dissatisfied, I'm Irish.

Robert Francis insists that there is a perfect symmetry in weather, life, and people:

> Ireland whose weather imitates
> bird flightiness, imitates life
> imitates above all the Irish.

Francis also recalls the curse and damage of "Cromwell," while David Cintino recalls the cruel contradictions of "Parnell." John Berryman finished his "Dream Songs" in Dublin, which thus plays its part as both source and setting for some of Henry's songs. Although Wallace Stevens never saw Ireland, his correspondence with Thomas McGreevy gave him the vision of the Ireland in "Our Stars Come from Ireland," a sense so strong that he told James Johnson Sweeney his idea of Ireland "would be diminished if he had seen the real thing."

The high modernist revolution of the early 20th century culminated in, arguably, the greatest poet and the greatest novelist of this century, Yeats and Joyce. Thus for most Irish-American poets some form of obeisance or rebellion has been almost obligatory. And so poems by James Schevill, Wendell Berry, and John Logan pay tribute to Yeats, while Nancy Sullivan and James McAuley balance praise with blame. John Logan and John Montague pay tribute to James Joyce, while Vicki Hearne ends this section with a "Soliloquy."

The sole Celts to avoid Roman conquest, the Irish have since the 9th century suffered centuries of other invasion and assimilation. Survival thus hinged on a sense of clan rather than country, of ancestor as antecedent, and so the Irish have been, and continue to be, an intensely tribal people, "the Indians of Europe" as Keith Wilson puts it. So also in America, the family group is particularly, and in an increasingly rootless and deracinated population, even peculiarly, important. The poetry of the third section reflects this primal preoccupation. Keith Wilson and Robert Creeley speak of moments of almost mystical racial recognition. Paul Carroll, Robert Kelly, Kathy Callaway, Galway Kinnell, Michael Heffernan, Terence Winch, Ann Darr, James Galvin, and Brendan Galvin all invoke parents and patterns of life of immediate forebearers. John Montague explores ancestral immigrant pains in "A Graveyard in Queens," while Eamon Grennan looks both toward the past and imagines the future of his children.

Since leaving is a fact of life on an island, return home has also been an elemental and ever-powerful theme in Irish-American poetry since often that journey had been delayed or denied. The fourth section organizes poems of two kinds: those American-Irish, either by birth or adoption, who have travelled to Ireland, and also the response of the Irish who have travelled to America. The responses range from playful to plaintive and encompass the mythic as well as the tourist.

Perhaps the first of these poetic travellers was Robinson Jeffers, who visited his wife's home in Northern Ireland in 1929 and produced a series of powerful and stony poems collected in *Descent to the Dead* (1931), and here represented by "Broadstone." Tess Gallagher hears the refrain "Cabbages and bones" in her stark "Ballad of Ballymote." Deborah Tall hauntingly recalls the "Island of the White Cow" and asks "Do we choose to leave as implausibly / as we choose to stay?" in her "Three Anecdotes." Michael Heffernan regains memory and a sense of place while Eugene Platt, "dreaming of Deirdres, Mauves / and a Nuala I may never know" reforms in "At Trinity College," and vows that his "projected major is monogamy."

In contrast and in exile rather than return, James McAuley describes a surreal response to a typically sentimental St. Patrick's Day in "Green Beer," while James Liddy hears the strange "Voice of America, 1961." Thomas Kinsella, echoing an early monastic scribe, responds to his "white exile" with a vow of "ever more painstaking care." The brilliant Irish feminist, Eavan Boland, seeks to imagine how "The Emigrant Irish"

> stood there, what they stood with
> that their possessions may become our power.

Dennis Maloney's "found" poem, "Letter from the Old Sod," ends this section on a similar recognition of the pains and process of passage.

The collection ends with eight first appearance poems generously offered up by five poets, by Irish-Americans Brendan Galvin, Paul Hogan and Keith Wilson and by Irish who respond to American myths about Ireland, James Liddy and John Montague.

> In making books of poetry
> every bugger gets his fee
> except the poet and the tree.

The aim of this collection is not, as in an ordinary anthology, "to collect and preserve the choice flowers of lyric fragrance and fineness" but instead to establish what Ezra Pound spoke of as an "active anthology" or as John Gross put it, "a book that sets ideas in motion and establishes a complex network of internal cross-references." Rather than establishing a canon in the old possessive, manipulative, "literature as commodity" tradition that Robert Graves and Laura Riding attacked, it is hope that this book will set minds and mouths in motion to examine, to celebrate, and, most importantly, to continue the artistic activity here presented as the Irish-American poem.

Historical/Legendary

SPENSER'S IRELAND

has not altered;—
   a place as kind as it is green,
   the greenest place I've never seen.
Every name is a tune.
Denunciations do not affect
     the culprit; nor blows, but it
is torture to him to not be spoken to.
They're natural,—
       the coat, like Venus'
mantle lined with stars,
buttoned close at the neck,—the sleeves new from disuse.

If in Ireland
   they play the harp backward at need,
   and gather at midday the seed
of the fern, eluding
their "giants all covered with iron," might
     there be fern seed for unlearn-
ing obduracy and for reinstating
the enchantment?
      Hindered characters
seldom have mothers
in Irish stories, but they all have grandmothers.

It was Irish;
   a match not a marriage was made
   when my great grandmother'd said
with native genius for
disunion, "Although your suitor be
     perfection, one objection
is enough; he is not
Irish." Outwitting
     the fairies, befriending the furies,
whoever again
and again says, "I'll never give in," never sees

that you're not free
   until you've been made captive by
   supreme belief,—credulity
you say? When large dainty
fingers tremblingly divide the wings
      of the fly for mid-July
with a needle and wrap it with a peacock-tail,
or tie wool and
         buzzard's wing, their pride,
like the enchanter's
is in care, not madness. Concurring hands divide

flax for damask
   that when bleached by Irish weather
   has the silvered chamois-leather
water-tightness of a
skin. Twisted torcs and gold new-moon-shaped
      lunulae aren't jewelry
like the purple-coral fuchsia-tree's. Eire—
the guillemot
         so neat and the hen
of the heath and the
linnet spinet-sweet— bespeak relentlessness? Then

they are to me
   like enchanted Earl Gerald who
   changed himself into a stag, to
a great green-eyed cat of
the mountain. Discommodity makes
      them invisible; they've dis-
appeared. The Irish say your trouble is their
trouble and your
         joy their joy? I wish
I could believe it;
I am troubled, I'm dissatisfied, I'm Irish.

Marianne Moore

4

OUR STARS COME FROM IRELAND

I
Tom McGreevy, in America, Thinks of Himself as a Boy

Out of him that I loved,
Mal Bay I made,
I made Mal Bay
And him in that water.

Over the top of the Bank of Ireland,
The wind blows quaintly
Its thin-stringed music,
As he heard it in Tarbert.

These things were made of him
And out of myself.
He stayed in Kerry, died there.
I live in Pennsylvania.

Out of him I made Mal Bay
And not a bald and tasselled saint.
What would the water have been,
Without that that he makes of it?

The stars are washing up from Ireland
And through and over the puddles of Swatara
And Schuylkill. The sound of him
Comes from a great distance and is heard.

II
The Westwardness of Everything

These are the ashes of fiery weather,
Of nights full of the green stars from Ireland,
Wet out of the sea, and luminously wet,
Like beautiful and abandoned refugees.

The whole habit of the mind is changed by them,
These Gaeled and fitful-fangled darknesses
Made suddenly luminous, themselves a change,
An east in their compelling westwardness,

Themselves an issue as at an end, as if
There was an end at which in a final change,
When the whole habit of the mind was changed,
The ocean breathed out morning in one breath.

Wallace Stevens

THE CELT

I heard a voice clang like a brass kettle clanging,
Voice of an Irish bricklayer haranguing
Some lesser bricklayers. His clapper-tongue
Jangled as when a bell is jarred not rung.
Only the tone—but I could understand
The bile and choler of his tragic land,
The Celtic turbulence, wrangling and war—
Things that had been mere history before.

Robert Francis

IRELAND

which the sea refuses
to recognize as bona fide
land, the sea and all her watery clouds

and all her mewing gulls
"white craws as white as snaw"
that sweep, that sweep, that sweep

warm winter into cool summer
"rather cloudy, but with bright
periods in many places this morning"—

Ireland whose weather imitates
bird flightiness, imitates life,
imitates above all the Irish.

Robert Francis

CROMWELL

After the celebrated carved misericords
And various tombs, the amiable sexton
Shows you by St. Mary's door the stone
Where Cromwell's men sharpened their swords.

Was it not a just, a righteous, war
When indiscriminate Irish blood
Flowed for the greater glory of God
Outside St. Mary's door?

If righteousness be often tipped with steel,
Be rightly tipped, psalm-singing men
Will help themselves to holy stone
To whet their zeal.

So you have both: the mellow misericords
Gracing the choir
And just outside the door
The swords.

Robert Francis

WHY IS IRELAND THE WETTEST PLACE ON EARTH
(#290)

Why *is* Ireland the wettest place on earth
year-round, beating Calcutta in the monsoon
& the tropical rain-forest?
Clearly the sun has made an exception for Ireland,
the sun growled & shone elsewhere: Iowa,
detestable State.

Adorable country, in its countryside
& persons, & its habits, & its past,
martyrs & heroes,
its noble monks, its wild men of high pride
& poets long ago, Synge, Joyce & Yeats,
and the ranks from which they rose.

Detestable State, made of swine & corn,
rich & ignorant, pastless, with one great tree in it
& doubtless certain souls
perplexed as the Irish whether to shout or mourn
over man's riddling fate: alter, or *stet:*
Fate across all them rolls.

John Berryman

THE IRISH SKY IS RAINING, THE IRISH WINDS ARE HIGH (#292)

The Irish sky is raining, the Irish winds are high,
the Irish sun comes back & forth, and I
in my Irish pub
past puberty & into pub-erty
have sent my Irish wife & child downtown,
I lapse like an Irish clown.

I dream, and God knows Henry's dreams are vivid
as the horses in Poona, lustrous on the track
whose father will not swim back
ruined in a grave in Oklahoma
loveless except for Henry steept in Homer
& Timon & livid.

Henry, who was always a crash programme,
smiled, and the smile was worse than the rictus of the victim,
'Another drop' said Mick.
He put his silver down, he took back all his lies,
he went down chimneys under the Irish skies
& the last voice in drawled; 'Henry? a brick,'

John Berryman

THE IRISH HAVE THE THICKEST ANKLES IN THE WORLD (#299)

The Irish have the thickest ankles in the world
& the best complexions. Unnerved by both,
Henry reserved his vote.
A dreadful dream, me stranded on a red rock slope
unable to go up, or down, or sideways:
shout for the Fire Department?

Your first day in Dublin is always your worst.
I just found my fly open: panic! A depressing
& badly written letter, very long,
from northern California enclosing a bad poem.
Fear of proving unworthy to my self-imposed task.
Fear.

And how will this last day in Dublin be,
away so many labours?— Offer up prayers,
Mr. Bones. Down on your knees.
Life comes against   not all at once but in layers.
—You offers me this hope. Now I thank you,
depressed, down on my knees.

John Berryman

PARNELL

You would never have got young men to sacrifice themselves for so unlucky a country as Ireland only that they pictured her as a woman.—Charles Stewart Parnell

In the Queen's cellar at Eltham
the alchemist broods over books
on mechanical engineering, mining,
delivers painful speeches to spiders
in an American voice thin as ringing silver,
amplified by mother's hatred
of antecedence and peasants.

A lord too shy to collect his rents,
he shocks a ghostly country with
wild superstition:
Beware of 13. Wear Nothing Green.
Blinded in Kilkenny, leading
a squad of goons to buy back
United Ireland, he dreams himself
sleepwalking into her room,
takes Healy's hand and calls him "Son."

He sleeps soundly on that last passage
from Holyhead to Kingstown pier,
wakes in time to accept a wreath
from his red-headed mistake.
"He's living," the red cabmen whisper
beyond the dark of Michan's, seeing
new lights in a troubled sky.

Pigott's letter, Carey's Irish sin
never touched you, lover:
but your mother going up in flame,
a country that slept with other men;
killed by contradiction, by what
you needed, what needed you.

David Cintino

THE SHY MAN

The full moon was shining upon the broad sea;
I sang to the one star that looked down at me;
I sang to the white horse that grazed on the quay—
   As I walked by the high sea-wall.
     But my lips they,
     My lips they,
   Said never a word,
   As I moped by the high sea-wall.

The curlew's slow night song came on the water.
That tremble of sweet notes set my heart astir,
As I walked beside her, the O'Connell's daughter,
   I knew that I did love her.
     But my lips they,
     My lips they,
   Said never a word,
   As we walked by the high sea-wall.

The full moon has fallen, the night wind is down
And I lie here thinking in bleak Bofin town
I lie here and thinking, 'I am not alone.'
   For here close beside me is O'Connell's daughter,
     And my lips they, my lips they,
     Say many a word,
   As we embrace by the high sea-wall.
     O! my lips they, my lips they,
     Say many a word,
   As we kiss by the high sea-wall.

Theodore Roethke

Literary

FOR THE OLD YEATS

The great ripping goes on in all minds,
A tearing of structure, a change;
Piercing through our loves, we find new loves,
Bodies alter in tidal lash of blood,
We are lost, we are found, we are alone.
In that loneliness, a stony center begins,
The hardening of age; lechers of time
We cling to a core of name, ancestral,
But skin changes, stiffens, hair whitens.
Who is that foolish, fond, ridiculous, old man?
Many years ago he was young and ran
His leaping, curving course.
Limping, he enters the noose of time,
Dreaming a fancy of love firm to hold,
And hangs there in his old, ludicrous hope
To the bawdy laughter of the world.

James Schevill

YEATS, RIVETED TO REVISIONS

Did Yeats, as dyslexic, write *"Hell"*
On the page as enigmatic, agonizing *"Yell"*?
As a ten-year-old dyslexic once said:
"What's wrong with me is just my words.
I can think ok, but I can't manage words."
The dyslexic writes, *"basgetti and cheese,"*
"Please up hurry," and *unclear* for *nuclear,*
Antagonistic poetry breaking language apart,
So Yeats, riveted to painful revisions,
Created essential structure through disorder,
Metaphors of possibility shining wonder
Out of the beast's inviting, oracular mouth.

James Schevill

TO WILLIAM BUTLER YEATS

All that we did, all that we said or sang
Must come from contact with the soil, from that
Contact everything Antaeus-like grew strong.
—"The Municipal Gallery Revisited"

Our kind vandalize the earth,
And yet you give me hope, your truth

The truth of change, and of the soil,
The changer, whose long toil

In summer sun and winter rain
Brings the fallen up again.

When your flesh became a shade,
Annihilated into what it made

And into earth, food for worms,
Substance exfoliating forms,

Poet, you were but keeping faith
With your native truth and place.

Dead, we will come back again
As beasts or worse or better men.

To no truth but change belong
The joy and burden of our song.

Wendell Berry

FOR W.B. YEATS
FROM ONE WHO NEVER MADE YOUNG MEN
CATCH THEIR BREATH WHEN SHE WAS PASSING

Ah Yeats, you're full of peat and dyes.
The greenery of Ireland has made you see
All ladies as lovelies with blue eyes.
No young man ever caught his breath at me
When I passed by, sooty-haired
With eyes the color of an unprized marble.
No young man swooned, caught his breath,
Or even coughed. Yeats, you're from the
      dreamer's land.

And were a fool. All ladies are not
Golden-haired with sapphire eyes.
Maude Gonne was one in twenty
When you were young and foolish
Down in those salley gardens.
She conned you into bombing a poet's larder:
The post office, the library. She told lies.
Well, no young man ever caught his breath
When I passed by, and things rip
At the seams as well as in the center.

Nancy Sullivan

20

TO AUSTIN CLARKE

William Butler Yeats is dead,
Patrick Kavanaugh gone to his reward.
Old poets, young poets, poets,
Honor Austin Clarke.

He walks alone in Ireland,
Black hat, muffler, greatcoat,
Threadbare buttonholes,
Pale eyes smiling, white hair
Drifting down like smoke in a heavy day.
It is left to him
To be the tongue of Ireland.
Listen to him at the last.

"I've no quarrel with the poets.
I've outlived nearly all my old friends.
Most of them died of drink.
I was saved by a weak stomach.
Many of the younger ones have gone to America
To teach, to live. I've stayed here.

"I've no quarrel with the Church.
The Archbishop is an able man.
There are many able men in the Church.
There must be for it to last.

"I've no quarrel with the government.
Poets are not censored in Ireland.
Playwrights, novelists, yes.
Not poets. Indifference, perhaps.
Irish Broadcasting treats me well.
They pay me even when I don't go on.

"Once as a boy
I climbed the wall at Coole Park.
Through the trees, I saw Yeats, walking.
It was wonderful.

"Poets don't know much, but they try.
They try every way; blind as bats
And deaf as well, they fly.
They carve stone with bone,
Form steel with sand.
They fight like small boys
With their eyes shut.
Crying before they are hurt, but brave."

Eugene McCarthy

AT DRUMCLIFFE CHURCHYARD, COUNTY SLIGO

1
That great feather the mind's wind drives
over the graves
and which lights
and stays on the tomb of Yeats
is make of skin and of thin stone
akin to cliff, akin to drum.

2
On this ancient monastic spot
I feel the shocks of rhythm underfoot—
gigantic hooves of heaving
Irish horses, their riders weaving
with ecstacy as their long, god-like legs
stretch
      and cleave tight
breaking up the patterning of light
the brown,
      the black, the roan,
the mottled hides give off
like the sun shining (and then not)
through mist
      in bursts
along Ben Bulben's back. The wild long-
haired man and the wild
long-haired woman ride
and merge and are gone.

3
Yeat's grave lifts to heaven
the body of a man, body of a woman—
himself, his wife, himself,
and his ambiguous epitaph
celebrates his birth forever back into life.
The great "cold eye" now opens
in the soaring brow of Man-Woman.

4

This gravesite is a bridge of sex.
It is a bridge of space
between
        the valley and the mountain—
between the long, free
flanks of the land and the fossil sea.
It is a bridge of time, for the round
stone tower still stands
where the medieval monks hovered
over the church cloths and silver
when the swift, marauding Vikings came.
And the Celtic rock High Cross
(figuring how Christian love
joins Adam and Eve
while
        Cain's hate kills Abel)
is raised along the selfsame
wall where a prehistoric standing stone
covered with its weathered skin
tapers hard toward the moon and sun,
its erect substance teeming full
of the tiny bright seed of shells.

5

Oh, I can feel the mind's wind blow still
over the graves, the church and Ben Bulben hill.
Wait! Touch your cheek!
For this feather breath breathes too
upon you.

                    for John Unterecker

John Logan

DUBLIN SUITE: HOMAGE TO JAMES JOYCE

I
The Bridge

It is raining. The child is waiting
for alms on the O'Connell Bridge in
Dublin. An infant cries in her arms.
She stays on the walk morning til night.
The child's eyes are hard. They're almost wild.

Her face is dirty as her dress is.
It is raining. The child is waiting.
The lid of a cardboard box for coins
begins to come apart in the wet.
Many of us pass her by. We fail

to tell how bone thin is her red shawl.
The infant she enwraps weighs heavy
in her small lap, and I tell you they
both lie *here* in the laps of us all.
It is raining. The child is waiting.

Joyce would have watched an epiphany.
His family was constantly poor.
It is Stephen's young sister who sits here.

II
The Library

This massive, carved medieval harp of Irish Oak
no longer sounds in the winds from the ancient times gone out
of Celtic towns. It rests in the long, high vaulted room
filled up with one million books whose pages chronicle
the works and ages both in *our* land and in Ireland.
For a hundred years no student has bent here above
those huge, leather volumes that burgeon on the balconies
like matched and stacked rows of great pipes
for the unplayed organ of this magnificent place.
But both pipes and harp seem still to come alive and turn
Trinity College Library
into a fantastic temple when we stand over

the twelfth-century Book of Kells,
which James Joyce so loved he carried a facsimile
to Zurich, Rome, Trieste. "It is,"
he said to friends, "the most purely Irish thing we have.
You can compare much of my work
to the intricate illuminations of this book."
Its goatskin pages open up for us under glass
in a wooden case. At this place:
a dog nips its tail in its mouth,
but this dog of ultramarine, most expensive
pigment after gold, for it was ground out of lapis,
and the tail is of the lemon yellow orpiment.
Other figures are verdigris, folium or woad—
the verdigris, made with copper,
was mixed with vinegar, which ate into the vellum
and showed through on the reverse page.
Through the text's pages run constant, colored arabesques
of animated initial
letters—made of the bent bodies
of fabulous, elongated beasts
linked and feeding beautifully upon each other,
or upon themselves. Why, even the indigo-haired
young man gnaws at his own entrails.
The archetypal figure of the uroboros
recurs, as does that the Japanese call *tomoi*:
a circle divided by three arcs from its center.
These illuminations around
the Irish script of the Gospels
are some of them benign and terrible like that
Satan from the four temptations:
the devil is black, a skeleton with flaming hair
and short, crumpled emaciated wings, which appear
to be charred as are the bony feet—
and the reptile with such gentle
eyes is colored kermes (compounded from the dried bodies
of female ants that die bright red).
The covers of jewels and gold are gone from the Book,
stolen for a while from the Kells
Monastery in County Meath
and then found, some of its gorgeous pages cut apart
and the whole stuffed beneath the sod.
These designs were all gestures of the bold minds of monks—
their devils still whirring about their ears while angels

26

blasted their inner eyes with colors not in any
spectrum, and moaning, primitive Celtic gods still cast
up out of their hermetic interior lives strange figures
which we can all recognize as
fragments of our inhuman dreams:
all this is emblazoned here in the unimagined
and musical colors of a medieval church.
Ah, friend, look how this Book of Kells
pictures all our heavens, all our hells.

III
The Green

Up Grafton Street to Stephen's Green
(which young Dedalus thought his own)
I pass the street named Duke. There two of Joyce's favored
pubs still stand, and one of them holds
in a blank wall the red door of Leopold Bloom's home:
it bears the golden number eight
from the house razed on Eccles Street.
Bloom's and Joyce's friends still lift their glasses of stout.
Two doors down from the Green, Captain America's Inn
offers up burgers and cokes and
those Irish potatoes which once,
boiled, kept the families alive,
but here are prepared like the French.
At the entrance to Stephen's Green
an Irish musician keens
on his pipes that wail like a child,
and the beautiful Irish coins
designed by friends of Yeats (dolphins grace and unplayed harps
adorn) are tossed into his cap,
which matches exactly the scarlet tartan of his kilt.
Gray couples walk or rest on benches and some young men
lounge on the Green with girls who hitch up their skirts and sun
their thighs, while other silent men
go in and out of the latrine again and again.
Students listen to the red-and-gold clad band
play from the raised circular stand
and eat their lunch before heading back across the street
to school. Most go round the corner south to UCD
or back down Grafton Street where Trinity College waits,

but some still stroll across to Newman Hall
where Joyce followed Hopkins and Cardinal Newman too.
Gerard Manley Hopkins (who saw things through drops of blood)
agonized here in this garden
as Christ in his Gethsemane—
he tried to decide even to the eighth of a point
the marks for the students he loved.
(Without high grades the Catholics
could not go to school in England.)
I see him there, lean, at his lecture stand in the hall.
On the Green his and Joyce's and Newman's steps still fall.
They mingle with ours like voices
or like the shouts of the great God-in-the-streets that's Joyce's.

IV
The Tower

I stand at the round parapet
of Joyce's Martello Tower.
I look over where the awkward, naked boys holler
and dive in the swimming place called "the forty-foot hole,"
since Joyce's time only for men, though now some militant has
        scrawled
in chalk at the entrance to the spot a woman's sign:
The Venus Mirror. I wonder
then: did *she* ever think of this?
Imagine Botticelli's figure (with her long, brown
strands) scrambling about those rocks amid angular kids.
How odd that sight. How odd this thought:
this tower was built in the fear of a French onslaught.
And this: Oliver St. John Gogarty paid the rent!
Certainly Joyce somehow did his share. The key's still there.
Huge, bronze, like the key of a king.
With it young Stephen unlocked the secrets of the heart,
but it was Joyce's hand the key
touched and taught. And there, down the long, curving iron stair
is Joyce's cane inside a glass case, and there's his watch,
his eyepatch, the memory of him—head in both hands—
struggling with the blindness of Homer. Or of Milton.
It is as if poets were forced to see inside themselves:
fall out of that insular tower of ignorance.
Tiresias, also blind, held up Venus' Mirror

and the Dart of Mars. Whatever man or woman dared
he did, he knew. There is no poet like that seer
as is Joyce, who was Molly and Leopold too. Jung
wrote him, "You know many things we psychologists don't—
especially about women."
Your cane, Joyce! Your key! The imprint of your foot on stone!
And your folded waistcoat fading there in closed case.
On it in blue, brown the woven hounds chase the fox.
Or do those hounds that heaved when your body breathed, hunt
    deer.
I feel the chase inside my chest,
here. Joyce, I feel I wear your vest—
and like you am more than human.
I too have within myself the boy, man and woman.
But your clothes make my heart inflate,
for that is not 'more than human.'
Why, Diana had the hunter who desired her
transformed into a deer, his flesh rent by his own dogs.
How often has the woman punished the man in her?
Or the man the woman in him?
How often have both choked back as they became adult
the boy or girl who wept in them
(although its sight was not the less).
Joyce, here in this tower with its enigmatic patch
for your omniscient eye, I
see better too. Women have taken up and used with strength
the chalk of men. And those have the teats of a girl.
Now, from your tower's top, let the pen-
nants of all our humankind unwind.

                    for Peter Logan
                    —1977

John Logan

29

JAMES JOYCE

Under the dented hat
with high black band;

that long face, sloping
like a gable down
to the jutting jaw;
sallow skin, scant
moustache, swallowed

by dark sudden-
ly glinting glasses

those slender fingers
cramped around a
walking stick or
white wine glass;
it could be my

father or yours;
any worn, life

tempered man if
the caption lacked
the detail—bright as
heresiarch or fallen
angel—of his name.

John Montague

LETTER TO RICHARD HUGO FROM DRUMCLIFF

Dear Dick, This kind of travel is cheap enough:
Hard a'starboard after a vexing nightmare,
And there I leave you—Mister Yeats at Coole,
Being severe with young poets on Lady Gregory's lawn,
Looking over his specs at a few bedraggled sheep
On the shore of the murky lake. And he counting them swans...

It's just a Byzantine canter through Roscommon,
A fearful country for tinkers, to Drumcliff.
A Philip Larkin chapel, half-buried in old trees;
Bland, tame Gothic of the Established Faith
That none of the neighbours give a damn about,
Keeping to their long-lipped superstitions,
Their guttural gossip making a natural prey
Of the ancestral rector—'He's a nice man, *but*...'
Half-starved mongrels worrying a lame sheep.

The embattled cleric: patrolling his neat grounds,
Pondering his fingernails, the only
Clean set in the parish; preparing to preach mildly
On "Prudence" again, to his congregation of five—
Six, if you counted the deafmute poorhouse orphan,
His only convert, who rang the Communion bell
And pulled the thistles from the gentry's graves.

The peasantry: He sang them plain and cruel,
Dour and quaint; went sour on them, invented
A freckled ghost in tweed with a fly-rod and an ear
Cold enough to hear him out. He caught
Neither salmon nor trout himself; hated low bars;
His women all had double-barrelled names.
How could *we* move in *his* circles? His goddam gyres!

Randy laughter, hell! His lightest rhyme
Was strictly Big House—a bronze gong embossed
With gyres, moon-phases, rose, rood, and tower;
Struck well, that great gong calls the lords and ladies
To their places at stage centre, *right*. He warped

The local colours of old saga, older *rann*,
To his own passionate, visionary weft,
As Vergil had for Rome in *her* decline.
Here, beneath white gravel, his immortal, bone-white grin.

There's an old cross at the top of the graveyard lane.
The disproportionate head of the crucified figure
Wears the same dissembling agony-smile.
Some nameless monk, ten centuries ago,
Chipped the lichen off a great rock and cut
Him down to size.
So, that gorgeous gong resounds through Idaho:
Here, the tourist looks up from the arrogant plain stone
To a rock flapping in a galebent oak. It's like
Getting pissed off at Xerxes, as you say. Best, Jim.

James J. McAuley

32

SOLILOQUY OF THE IRISH POET

My singing moves the wind, the seeking of swift horses
Does not thrill the earth so, I wear the six
Colors in my coat. The seventh, for king's death,
Encumbers all but me. The drumming of wild hooves,
The fright of all who have been spared by the great
Mild mercy of horses, the flimsy call of flat birds
Against the summer thunder, the thunder itself,
And earthquakes, the earth trembling to knowledge
As the huge harps tremble to the light fingers
Of girls, the invocations of priests like sweet oil
Scenting the stones of churches, and the great bells'
Reverberations are but flax for my linen and forms
For my flight. I wear the six colors, the last,
Scarlet for the king's death, is hid in cunning
Threads inside the seams, binding him, freeing me.

Vicki Hearne

33

Family

THE CELT IN ME

In a museum here I saw a Celtic swordblade,
rusted, bent in combat. No handle.
These men who built what now are shadowed ruins,

my ancestors; from deathmasks, carvings
I see similar features. Gaiety, defiance,
Lost causes, futile wars. Indians of Europe.

Always the High Goddess, Moon Lady of White
streaming with light with eyes that touch
as the breeze moves through the Holy Tree.

From ancient barrows, dim men with old robes
walk gravely through the Danube mists
their arms outstretched for me.

Keith Wilson

THERESA'S FRIENDS

From the outset charmed
by the soft, quick speech
of those men and women,
Theresa's friends—and the church

she went to, the "other,"
not the white plain Baptist
I tried to learn God in.
Or, later, in Boston the legend

of "being Irish," the lore, the magic,
the violence, the comfortable
or uncomfortable drunkenness.
But most, that endlessly present talking,

as Mr. Connealy's, the ironmonger,
sat so patient in Cronin's Bar,
and told me sad, emotional stories
with the quiet air of an elder

does talk to a younger man.
Then, when at last I was twenty-one,
my mother finally told me
indeed the name *Creeley* was Irish—

and the heavens opened, birds sang,
and the trees and the ladies spoke
with wondrous voices. The power of the glory
of poetry—was at last mine.

Robert Creeley

MOCKERY AGAINST THE IRISH CENSORSHIP

Ireland was better in its dream,
with the oppressor foreign.
Now its art leaves home to keen
and its voice is orange.
It is a sad revolt, for loving's health,
that beats its enemy and then itself.

Now that Irishmen are free
to enslave themselves together
they say that it is better they
do worst to one another
then have the english do them good
in an exchange of joy for blood.

A just as alien pius blacks
their greens of lovers' commerce;
rehearsing victory, they lack
a government to fill its promise.
Worse, law has slacked the silly harp
that was their once and only Ark

out, and I am sorry to be flip
and narrowly disrespectful,
but since I wade at home in it
I stoop and take a mouthful
to splatter the thick walls of their heads
with American insult! Irish sense is dead.

Alan Dugan

ON BEING OUT-CLASSED BY CLASS

You	Where I came from is torn down,
say,	where I'm at is condemned,
"You	and where I'm going to
can't	is not built up yet. My Grand
be	Father steamed away from yours
any	for eats! regards! and joys.
good	Better to be Dugan the Cop
because	and never talk about a shitty past
you	than to be chased out
aren't	of the potatoes in the old
some	sod. He dreamed America up, and I
one	played Indian against
from	his cowboy lies because:
some	tradition is for the rich
place."	to love, the clerks
Ha!	to ape, the poor
	to suffer, so I wander
	to take the air, regards, and joys.
	Where are they? You
	will tell me. Anyone
	free of your slavery
	is better off in his own,
	so Up the five-hour day!
	Up art! Up the I.R.A.!

Alan Dugan

FATHER

How sick
I get of your ghost.
And of always looking at this tintype on my desk
of you as a cocky kid:
Kilkenney's coast, rocks and suncracked turf
giving the resilience to your countenance
as you try to seem so nonchalant, posing
in a rented Sunday morning suit,
spats and bowler hat:
a greenhorn off the boat. And yet,
something in that twist of fist,
knuckles taut about the cane knob, shows
how you already seem to know
you'll transform that old cow pasture of Hyde Park
into your own oyster.

The way you did.

And that other photo
stuck somewhere in my dresser
drawer
amid the Xmas handkerchiefs
the rubbers, poems
and busted rosary beads:
Posed beneath three palmtrees
on Tampa Beach's boardwalk,
a stocky man who'd made his millions by himself;
and could quarrel with Congressmen in Washington
about the New Deal bank acts;
or call Mayor Kelly crooked to his face.

Hair,
bone, cock,
face and skin, brains:
rotten in the earth these 16 years.

Remember, father, how Monsignor Shannon
(whose mouth you always said
looked exactly like a turkey's ass)
boomed out Latin above your coffin at Mount Olivet?
                    But as the raw October rain
                    rasped against our limousine
                    guiding the creeping cars back into
                            Chicago,
        Jack, your first born,
        picked his nose; and
        for an instant flicked a look
to ask if I too knew you were dead for good—
                    St Patrick's paradise a club
                    for priests and politicians
                    you wouldn't get caught dead in.

        You used to like to call me Bill,
And kiss me. Take me to the Brookfield Zoo.
        Or stuff English toffee in my mouth.
But always after you'd cursed
        and with a bedroom slipper
whacked the tar out of Jack.

                    This morning, father,
                    broke as usual,
                        no woman in my bed,
        I threw six bucks away
        for a shave and haircut at The Drake.
And looked again for you.
                    On Oak Street beach,
gazing beyond the bathers and the boats,
I suddenly searched the horizon, father,
            for that old snapshot of Picasso
                    and his woman Dora Maar.
        Picasso bald and 60;
but both in exaltation, emerging
                    with incredible sexual dignity
        from the waters of the Gulfe Juan.

                            Tattoo
                            of light
                            on lake.

Bleached spine of fish.

Those ripples of foam: semen of the ghost.

                              I left the lake;
                    but tripped in the quick dark
                    of the Division Street underpass;
then picked a way past newspaper scraps,
                         puddles and a puckered beachball.
                    I looked for dirty drawings on the wall.
          Traffic crunches overhead.
This underpass is endless.

Paul Carroll

A WOMAN FROM CONNAUGHT

My great-great-great-great-grandmother
on my father's father's father's mother's side
I remember with the curious vividness of all creatures.
She was small
and her perfectly round eyes had not yet
been lost in the big green slit-eyes lewdness of the Kelly eyes.
She travelled once in her long life down
from the north and west where her fathers
had been kings, and their wives and mothers
innocent harlots of sunshine,
paid by green life for all their travail,
wild sex of white-thighed women till she came along.

The exploits stopped then.
A long smouldering
match had reached at last her philosophic powder.
She exploded into a restless stillness,
read books in four languages, wore her round
eyes milky with cataract but still,
even at the last of things, thought she could see
the devoted moon go up
over the rafters of her slatternly house,
all dim spiders and dirt floors she guessed.
But the floors were good oak parquet
and her own bees made the wax that gleamed
high over her mind in the white rooms.

Their echo I still hear, rooms or bees,
song of their summing
all the names and numbers of the flowers
that writhed unseen in her garden. She was not sexy.
She thought things into place and held them there.
She could hardly tell if the candles were lit.

The skirts of her redingote trailed
at times across her feet. She thought them rats
and marvelled at their boldness,
wondered should she not be firmer with the servants,
if indeed those english-speaking shadows
were her servants, not mere ghosts
of all her enemies come back to mock

with unclear whispers at the edge of rooms.

The fields are always blank, she thought,
and autumn rebukes the summer's brashness.
It is empty. They are empty.
So blank there had to be a force somewhere
austere and honest. She called it God
and thought men ought to honor it
by books in many languages, and keeping still,
and sitting in large rooms alone.
                              Oh God
she prayed, keep the smell of the stables away.
Dont let me hear the wasps yawning all spring long.
Dont let me hear the children singing
or Sarah's petticoat slither on wet grass.
Let me know you in an Irish silence,
sweet dumb of heart & clever-mouth & loving.
Let there be nothing but love and then not even that.

But when the gardener mowed the lawns
the smell of the grass came
in the long windows and stood in the room like kings.
From her I have my love of cloudy days,
long pauses in the conversation, silences
at the ends of lines of poetry, thick symphonies,
quiet women and their heavy gods.

Robert Kelly

LOVE IN THE WESTERN WORLD

Think of family, Ulster Irish
run out on a ram's horn,
our first real move.
The same square hands
ploughing through Missouri
and Iowa and Minnesota,
where we learned to muffle
the cavities of the body,
batten the heart down
on loneliness. Still it beats
family, family, as if the pulse
of our one-to-a-body rivers
ever ran singular. And if nothing
continues—the body ending
in this fist, everything short
of the mark—what do we want?
Don't give me history. No bridges
from my heart to your heart
to all of them stringing back
like dark berries: only
open my hand, press it
for the feel of the river,
the old fishline unreeling again.

Kathy Callaway

GOODBYE

1

My mother, poor woman, lies tonight
in her last bed. It's snowing, for her, in her darkness.
I swallow down the goodbyes I won't get to use,
tasteless, with wretched mouth-water;
whatever we are, she and I, we're nearly cured.

The night years ago when I walked away
from that final class of junior high school students
in Pittsburgh, the youngest of them ran
after me down the dark street. "Goodbye!" she called,
snow swirling across her face, tears falling.

2

Tears have kept on falling. History
has taught them its slanted understanding
of the human face. At each last embrace the dying give,
the snow brings down its disintegrating curtain.
The mind shreds the present, once the past is over.

In the Derry graveyard where only her longings sleep
and armfuls of flowers go out in the drizzle
the bodies not yet risen must lie nearly forever...
"Sprouting good Irish grass," the graveskeeper blarneys,
he can't help it, "a sprig of shamrock, if they were young."

3

In Pittsburgh tonight, those who were young
will be less young, those who were old, more old, or more likely
no more; and the street where Syllest,
fleetest of my darlings, caught up with me
and hugged me and said goodbye, will be empty. Well,

one day the streets all over the world will be empty—
already in heaven, listen, the golden cobblestones have fallen still—
everyone's arms will be empty, everyone's mouth, the Derry earth.
It is written in our hearts, the emptiness is all.
That is how we have learned, the embrace is all.

Galway Kinnell

FIRST CONFESSION

Blood thudded in my ears. I scuffed,
   Steps stubborn, to the telltale booth
Beyond whose curtained portal coughed
   The robed repositor of truth.

The slat shot back. The universe
   Bowed down his cratered dome to hear
Enumerated my each curse,
   The sip snitched from my old man's beer,

My sloth pride envy lechery,
   The dime held back from Peter's Pence
With which I'd bribed my girl to pee
   That I might spy her instruments.

Hovering scale-pans when I'd done
   Settled their balance slow as silt
While in the restless dark I burned
   Bright as a brimstone in my guilt

Until as one feeds birds he doled
   Seven Our Fathers and a Hail
Which I to double-scrub my soul
   Intoned twice at the altar rail

Where Sunday in seraphic light
   I knelt, as full of grace as most,
And stuck my tongue out at the priest:
   A fresh roost for the Holy Ghost.

X.J. Kennedy

HANGOVER MASS

Of all the sins of the flesh, that reprobate
    My father had but one, and it had class:
To sip tea of a Sunday till so late
    We'd barely make it up to Drunkard's Mass.

After a sermon on the wiles of booze,
    The bread and wine transformed with decent haste,
Quickly the priest would drive us forth to graze
    Where among churchyard flocks I'd get a taste

Of chronic loneliness. Red-rimmed of eye,
    Quaking of hand, old men my old man knew
Would congregate to help bad time go by:
    Stout Denny Casey, gaunt Dan Donahue

Who'd mention girls with withering contempt,
    Each man long gone past hope to meet his match
Unless in what he drank all night, or dreamt.
    Each knee I stared at cried out for a patch.

A sealed half-pint, I'd stand there keeping mum
    Till, bored to death, I'd throw a fit of shakes.
Then with relief we'd both go stepping home
    Over sidewalk cracks' imaginary snakes.

X.J. Kennedy

COMING OF AGE ON THE HARLEM
for Kathy

I

My father would tie a life jacket
to a length of seaworn rope and dangle me
off the dock of The Harlem Boat Club float.
A strange baptism.
Down, down into the mad rushing river,
worm on a hook, a girl of six or seven,
I am let loose among water rats,
made sister to half-filled soda cans
floating vertically home from a picnic,
and to condoms that look like mama doll socks
in the unopened infant eye.
What man would toss his child to that swill?
He who can swim across the river,
whose arms churn a feud with the current.
He thinks he can hold me from any maelstrom.
Safe on the dock, I watch my father
float on his back from the Bronx
to Manhattan and back again.

II

Between the river edge and river park,
the New York Central tracks could fry a child.
How lucky to have this father with
long, strong arms to whisk me over
the wooden hooded, menacing third rail.
Can you remember when you reached your father's waist
and he told you of the serpent track where
only birds could land in safety?
But one day my father takes me home a different way:
up the wooden bridge above the tracks
where huge phallic shapes have been burned in black
along its walls. Don't look. Don't look.
That sight will fry you up like Semele.
Now my strong father, my never ruffled father
pulls me roughly over the wooden planks.

His dark face reddened tells of great,
unspoken danger. When we reach the street,
he makes me promise never to come this way again,
never to go to the river shore without him.
Over my shoulder I form an opposite determination.

III

The Harlem Boat Club is the man place.
My father slips down twice a week to shower,
on weekends plays a sweaty game
of four wall ball. Outside in the garden,
I wander six years old among lilies
of the valley, Queen Anne's lace,
the shoreline irises and great climbing rose
that began as someone's potted plant.
Elmer, the muscular black cat,
drags a water rat to the front door.
I follow inside to the boat room,
run my hand along the lean flanks
of polished rowing sculls,
then up the stairway, pause at the wooden roster,
the names with gold stars dead in some war.
Then the sweat smell of the lockers,
the place where they held a party
to welcome the Beatty brothers home from Korea.
Off to the side, three men stand
naked in the steamy, tiled shower.
Quiet, I sit down on a bench
beside a girl my own age, who has also come
to pretend she doesn't notice.

IV

Still my close, though distant, friend,
who sat with me in the men's locker room,
whose father had a strong right arm for handball,
whose mother and mine embarrassed
in their forties, had pregnancies,
who accompanied me through puberty
up and down the Harlem shore,

Kathy, in your Brahmin home in Brooklyn,
you say you want to rid your sleep
of those dirty years along the river.
But stop for a moment, stop trying
to make the river pass genteelly,
for there'll be no weaning from those waters.
Instead come back with me and watch
the sun glint off the rippling surface,
bearing the shore-hugging flow of turds and
condoms north to the Hudson.
You conjectured it all came from cabin cruisers
on some far-off glory ocean.
Kathy, would you have even looked
if you had known it came from humble tenements
on our Highbridge hill?
Could that one reflection
have darkened all your plans to sail?

V

"Mirror Mirror"
was the name you gave him,
a dexterous man with a pocket mirror
who could catch the Sunday morning sun
and flash it on our untouched child bodies.
A fairy tale gone haywire, Rapunzel in reverse:
"Mirror Mirror!"
we shouted from the bridge height,
and he below us in the river park
would hold his instrument to the sky like
a sextant and calculate his grotesque angles.
Then we'd race down the ramp
just beyond his unknown reach and dive
behind the safety of a tree.
Oh God! Oh God! the heavy breathing,
ours, his, the fear, the vague desire
that was always escaped in time to
run home at one for Sunday dinner and meet our
unsuspecting fathers coming home from mass.

VI

Just before ten, just before your father's curfew,
you can station yourself on the highway bridge,
where it joins the ramp from the river park,
to see the couples rise up on the evening tide:
the sooty venuses with dirty hand marks
on white and fondled blouses, and
their boyfriends swaggering in teenage jeans.
You laugh, and send your first awakening lust
to follow them back to the neighborhood
where someday all will notice that you've grown.
And small children will stand on bridges
to flank your path
as you make your debut entry
to the nightly river park cotillion, on the arm
of some lanky boy with a dangling black curl,
and the cleanest, oh the cleanest hands.

VII

It's the boys with sprouts of pubic hair
who have the manliness to strip and jump
while tourists on the Circle Line around
Manhattan watch with Brownie cameras.
Bright faced fathers and mothers, pointing out
the river life to their wondering children.
They look for street kids in straw hats,
the Tom Sawyers and Huck Finns of the Harlem
but only get an upraised finger.
Behind the nude boys who perch on river rocks
and invite the sun to their members,
a ring of girls, in tight black shorts and
pony tails, keep a coy but glancing distance.
And behind them all, a white-haired voyeur
drops his pants to masturbate.
The eyes of the Circle Line sail up river, still
hopeful that Becky Thatcher in eyelet bloomers
will wave a hanky from the shore.

VIII

In Undercliff Park, below Washington Bridge,
I play stretch and toe-knee-chest-nut with
my father's pocketed army knife.
A dangerous age. Threats are cutting through the air:
the flailing depantsings, the groping bra quests for
a wad of cotton or a nylon stocking.
A dangerous age, with the deadly fear
of being found a child.
To relieve it one day, we hang a tire in a tree and
swing in packs out over the cliff edge, until
the boy beside me loses grip and lies below,
as quiet as an infant in a lullabye.
Weeks later, we visit him at home, sign his casts
and giggle at his immature pajamas.
He lifts his mattress to show
an arsenal of thirty knives and ice picks,
and lets each girl pick a pocket lighter
shoplifted from Woolworth's.

IX

Hung by my hands above water,
I am dangled by boys from the ledge
of the Washington Bridge abutment.
Twelve years old, twelve feet from the surface,
I do not trust boys, but love their giddy danger
like a windflaw teasing with a sail.
And while we dangle, the boys hurl rocks
at the river, waiting for the splash that will leap
up to our blouses and clutch the outlines
of our forming breasts.
Soaked through, we climb the naked limbs
of a shore tree and sprawl in the afternoon sun.
Above a boy hovers in the branches,
reaches for my hand a moment and is gone,
leaving something growing in me
that holds me separate from my friends
as we walk together to our fathers' houses,
wearing our secret scent of the river.

X

My husband no longer swims b.a.
I can no longer picture his shadow
rippling across the sidewalks to the Harlem.
A swaggering, older boy, once unattainable.
Now at night I cradle his black hair
to my breast and we share the river's secrets:
My splashing joyride pick-up
with three strange boys in a motor boat.
His first hesitating touch of Dodie, the hillbilly
girl on the fourteen steps below Macombs Dam Bridge.
The tales of all those years I was not permitted
at The Harlem, unless my father stood beside me,
gathering me into his safe garden.
All those years I learned the route to avoid his path.
Now I retrace it in the dark, step by step, till
again I watch The Harlem Boat Club burn,
and see the steps plucked from the river bridge
where no child can again take the path
that leads me nightly to this good bed.
Kathy, did we escape our fathers?
Or did they play our turns and detours
just carefully enough to lead us here?

Joan Murray

KENNEDY

One late afternoon I hitched from Galway down to Kinvara on the edge of the Burren, one of those long midsummer days when the sun labors at last out of all-day rain and sets very late in the evening. In dark pubs all up and down the street, the townsmen hunched to their pints, silent and tentative as monks at supper. Thinking to take my daily Guinness, I stopped, and Kennedy was there, his picture on the mantel behind the bar.

A black-headed citizen half in his cups sidled over and smiled. Ah Kennedy Kennedy, a lovely man, he said and brought me a Guinness. Ah yes, a lovely man, I said, and thank you very much. Yes Kennedy, and they slaughtered him in his youth the filthy communists, he said, and will you want another. Yes, slaughtered him in his youth, I said and thanked him very much.

All night till closing time we drank to Kennedy and cursed the communists—all night, pint after pint of sour black lovely stout. And when it came Time, I and my skin and the soul inside my skin, all sour and lovely, strode where the sun still washed the evening, and the fields lay roundabout, and Kinvara slept in the sunlight, and Holy Ireland, all all asleep, while the grand brave light of day held darkness back like the whole Atlantic.

Michael Heffernan

FATHERS

We talked to our Jamesons at closing time
about our fathers' last words. I said mine said,
Keep your nuts tight, meaning electric wire nuts,
and you said yours said, See you in April, boy.
Those were our two damn shames in Dublin that night.
We walked back and sang us a couple of damn shames.
I said I had drunk a little and felt good
and you said you were sober as you could be.
We tried to decide which was finer, the Champs
Elysées or O'Connell Street, but couldn't,
so we went to sleep discussing the fine points.
Out in the lamplight somebody kept yelling
to somebody else two or three blocks over
who yelled back once. It got quiet after that.

For Gibbons Ruark

Michael Heffernan

MY FATHER

my father died two years ago
but by then I had inherited
a great many things from him
he liked to take baths and so do I
he didn't like to go to the country
or the beach because it was uncomfortable
because of the bugs and sun, things like that
and I feel pretty much the same way
my father liked to have a good time
and so do I
he liked to go to parties and had
numerous friends who thought he was
the nicest person you'd ever want to meet
and he was the nicest person you'd ever
want to meet   he was generous and worked hard
and had a tendency to believe the best about people
(which didn't always work out best for him)
the only thing he read was the *Daily News*
but even so he was a natural pacifist
and when I got reclassified One A
and asked him what I should do after enumerating
my options one night when we were eating supper
back in sixty eight   he thought about it painfully
for about ten minutes during which time
I didn't say a word
and then he said "go to jail"
which was a very hard thing
for him to say
he learned to play the banjo by ear
and never got really good on it
though he could get by all right
and that's true of me too
another thing I inherited from my father
was his old Vega banjo with a shamrock pasted
on the skin which he gave me about five years ago
when he was too sick to play it any more

Terence Winch

HOME IN THE BRONX

I had my first real date with Barbara Liston
she was the younger sister of Nora Liston
who was the same age as my brother   Nora
was the same age as my brother and very popular
their mother died of cancer a year or two
before my mother   she came up to visit my
mother one night before she died to tell
my mother what it was like to have cancer
Mr. Liston was an inspector for the buses
me and Barbara went to the RKO Chester
to see *Two Women* starring Sophia Loren
we never went on another date after the first one
since even though I liked Barbara and thought
she was cute I was more interested in Pat
McCarthy   Barbara was upset by this
me and Pat went steady for nine months
we couldn't stand each other   when we made
out in her hallway I would make believe
I was interested in having sex and she
would make believe she wasn't   both of us
lied   she went to Rockaway for a month
I was home in the Bronx looking for
a summer job   I eventually got one playing
the drums in the Catskills   she called me up
and told me she was breaking off with me
and going steady with Bobby Swift
who was a friend of mine from school
Pat McCarthy wore thick girdles
I never got any idea what she really felt like

Terence Winch

A GRAVEYARD IN QUEENS
for Eileen Carney

We hesitate along
flower encumbered

avenues of the dead;
Greek, Puerto-Rican,

Italian, Irish—
(our true Catholic

world, a graveyard)
but a squirrel

dances us to it
through the water

sprinklered grass,
collapsing wreaths,

& taller than you
by half, lately from

that hidden village
where you were born

I sway with you
in a sad, awkward

(swelling the North
wind with groans,

curses, imprecations
against heaven's will)

but your mind is
a humble house, a

soft light burning
beneath the holy

dance of pain
over the grave of

my uncle & namesake—
the country fiddler—

& the grave of almost
all your life held,

your husband & son
all three sheltering

under the same
squat, grey stone.

*

You would cry out
against what has

happened, such
heedless hurt,

had you the harsh
nature for it

Oh, absurdity
of grief in that

doll's house, all
the chair legs sawn

to nurse dead children:
love's museum!

*

61

picture, the image
of the seven times

wounded heart of
her, whose portion

is to endure. For
there is no end

to pain, nor of
love to match it

& I remember Anne
meekest of my aunts

rocking & praying
in her empty room.

at the border
of this grave plot

serious, still,
a small ornament

holding something
a nut, a leaf—

like an offering
inside its paws.

*

For an instant
you smile to see

his antics, then
bend to tidy

flowers, gravel
like any woman

It sent me down
to the millstream

to spy upon a
mournful waterhen

slushing her young
along the autumn

flood, as seriously
as a policeman and

after scampering
along, the proud

plumed squirrel
now halts to stand

making a bed,
arranging a room,

over what were
your darlings' heads

and far from
our supposed home

I submit again
to stare soberly

at my own name
cut on a gravestone

& hear the creak
of a ghostly fiddle

filter through
American earth

the slow pride
of a lament.

John Montague

GAELIC LEGACY

1.

Trying to ignore the only thing
I can surely count on, Time,
        as a subject weeded and warted
        by every young twister of words,
        a phase I thought I could slip
        in a slippery apprenticeship
        (Modern Dancing with Miss Muse)
        whose leotard has been replaced
        with ruffled lace before I've reached
        the bottom of the page...
which brings me to my subject, space,
        a kind of time.

2.

Having a built-in Irish timing, oblique
as O'Cornered names (dear Great-grandmother
Sally O'Neil has fallen down the O'hill
and died next day with O'Chill and grandpa
was O'sued by his O'widow'O)
        While I knit such
        from a nonsense bush
        time has passed
        in a padded hearse
        with things I meant
        to say aboard.

3.

        Learning that I know
        what I have long known
        gives the effect of
        spending my life
        walking backward.

4.

And dear Great-grandmother Annie Trent
        cornered herself a century
            to become smaller
            and smaller in.
        String saved my life, she said,
        and at the end, For what?

Dear tender Annie Trent,
        le grande experiment.
Your string fenced out the savages
        who meant to do you in.
With exquisite knots you civilized
        your lace, our lives.

5.

Dear Father Hartke,
        How can man escape
            his animality?
                Why
        would he want to?

    Every morning he must
    push it away
            and put on
        his civilized socks.
                            Peace.

Ann Darr

LOOKING FOR ORIGINS

Here on the mountain the thistles
are riding their purple swath.
They translate into dollar signs
in town, prickly all the way.

If I could sell bread, I mean
a loaf I punched and muttered into,
and put in the right-temperatured oven,
I might survive and pay the rent,

but translation is always here.
Something into something else.
I keep thinking maybe a color will
survive, or a tune on a hollow reed.

I should know better.
Survival is for the fittest.
But I remember a man
who knew where he started. And told us

to start where we were. Someday I might
be able to do what he said.
He had conquered his thistles, his
purple. The loaf was in his head.

Ann Darr

ANTHROPOLOGY

Remember the night you got drunk
and shot the roses?
You were a perfect stranger, Father,
even my bad sister cried.

Some other gravity,
not death or luck,
drew fish out of the sea
and started them panting.

The fish became a man.
The archer's bow became a violin.
I remember the night you searched the sofa
for change

and wept on the telephone.
Some other gravity,
not time or entropy,
pulled the knife down for centuries.

The archers dropped their bows,
harmless as pine needles in the snow.
The knife became a plow
and entered the earth, Father.

Later it became a boat
and some other things—
It isn't a dream but it takes a long time,
for the archer's bow to become a violin.

James Galvin

A GENTLE ART

for my mother

I've been learning how to light a fire
Again, after thirty years. Begin (she'd say)
With a bed of yesterday's newspapers—
Disasters, weddings, births and deaths,
All that everyday black and white of
History is first to go up in smoke. The sticks
Crosswise, holding in their dry heads
Memories of detonating blossom, leaf. Saved
From the ashes of last night's fire.
Arrange the cinders among the sticks.
Crown them with coal nuggets, handling
Such antiquity as behooves it,
For out of this darkness, light. Look,
It's a cold but comely thing
I've put together as my mother showed me,
Down to sweeping the fireplace clean. Lit
You must cover from view, let it concentrate—
Some things better done in secret.
Pretend another interest but never
Let it slip your mind: know its breathing.
Its gulps and little gasps, its silence
And satisfied whispers, its lapping air.
At a certain moment you may be sure (she'd say)
It's caught. Then you simply let it be.
It's on its own now, leading its mysterious
Hungry life, becoming more itself by the minute,
Like a child grown up, growing strange.

Eamon Grennan

67

TAKING MY SON TO SCHOOL

His first day. Waiting, he plays
By himself in the garden.
I take a photo he clowns for,
Catching him, as it were, in flight.

All the way there in the car he chatters
And sings, giving me directions.
There are no maps for this journey:
It is the wilderness we enter.

Around their tall bespectacled teacher,
A gaggle of young ones in summer colours.
Silent, he stands on their border,
Clutching a bunch of purple dahlias.

Shyly he offers them up to her.
Distracted she holds them upside down.
He teeters on the rim of the circle,
Head drooping, a flower after rain.

I kiss him goodbye and leave him:
Stiff, he won't meet my eye.
I drive by him but he doesn't wave.
In my mind I rush to his rescue.

The distance bleeding between us,
I steal a last look back:
From a thicket of blondes, brunettes,
His red hair blazes.

It is done. I have handed him over.
I remember him wildly dancing
Naked and shining, shining
In the empty garden.

Eamon Grennan

POTSO, MY WINE-DARK UNCLE

I incarcerate you behind
that door with cracked panels,
padlock you at the back of my mind
and throw the key away, until
an evening spills the buttermilk of lethargy
across heights of its going,
and you knock quietly as
the shadow of a whisper you were
at every gathering of the clan.
You are trying to enter, dapper to pointy shoes,
inviting me to give up everything
and follow you, to circle the parking lot
at Mooney's Funeral Home where you've
outlasted temperate sisters like some
dwarf who knows the game by name.
You pencil the winning greyhounds,
even with guts half shot
planning another jaunt to Wonderland.
But you were no original.
Everyone I know had one like you,
and nobody wanted to stumble into your footsteps.
At fifty-five you ran away from home
with a trumpet player's glue-faced wife.
After your ice-cream ride,
for your nacre-button suit and double-breasted
henchman's overcoat, your nephews
raced your landlord up four flights
to a room the smell and color of
an empty mustard jar.

Brendan Galvin

JUST IN CASE YOU'RE WONDERING WHO YOU ARE

I am your little grandmother,
thief of the Queen's trout,
more oak and vinegar
than Mammy Yokum, but cold
as my white hair knot
for fear babies will grow
only as tall as typhus.

I keep the store in
the corner cellar, pick up
an acre here or there
like patchwork, and nurse
my forest people's paranoia.

My father's the one
whose skull's like
a scratched cobble
from trying to figure
how he dug a canal
and turned rocks into soil
with his Irish slide-rule.

After our trees fell down
and sailed away, our fields
fell down each year
and sailed away. With help
my father's house fell down
the day before the landlord
shook us off the estate
like crumbs from his shirtfront.
We followed the trees
and fields to Liverpool.

Brendan Galvin

in my dream

in my dream   my grandmother
maggie sullivan   has me by
both shirt sleeves   & is
agitating me up & down   "Use
Gerunds!"   she is screaming

Maureen Owen

Travel/Exile/Return

THE BROADSTONE

Near Finvoy, County Antrim

We climbed by the old quarries to the wide highland of
    heath,
On the slope of a swale a giant dolmen,
Three heavy basalt pillars upholding the enormous slab,
Towers and abides as if time were nothing.
The hard stones are hardly dusted with lichen in nobody
    knows
What ages of autumns in this high solitude
Since a recordless tribe of an unknown race lifted them up
To be the availing hero's memorial,
And temple of his power. They gathered their slighter dead
    from the biting
Winds of time in his lee, the wide moor
About him is swollen with barrows and breaks upon many
    stones,
Lean gray guardians of old urned ashes,
In waves on waves of purple heather and blithe spray of its
    bells.
Here lies the hero, more than half God,
And nobody knows his name nor his race, in the bee-bright
    necropolis,
With the stone circle and his tribe around him.
Sometimes perhaps (but who'd confess it?) in soft adoles-
    cence
We used to wonder at the world, and have wished
To hear some final harmony resolve the discords of life?
—Here they are all perfectly resolved.

Robinson Jeffers

THE BALLAD OF BALLYMOTE

We stopped at her hut
on the road to Ballymote
but she did not look up
and her head was on her knee.

What is it, we asked.
As from the dreams of the dead
her voice came up.

My father, they shot him
as he looked up from his plate
and again as he stood and again
as he fell against the stove
and like a thrush his breath
bruised the room
and was gone.

A traveler would have asked directions
but saw she would not lift her face.
What is it, he asked.

My husband sits all day in a pub
and all night and I may as well
be a widow for the way he beats me
to prove he's alive.

What is it, asked the traveler's wife,
just come up to look.

My son's lost both eyes in a fight
to keep himself a man
and there he sits behind the door
where there is no door

and he sees by the stumps
of his hands.

And have you no daughters for comfort?

Two there are and gone to nuns
and a third to the North
with a fisherman.

What are you cooking?

Cabbage and bones, she said. Cabbage
and bones.

Tess Gallagher

THE WAY WEST

I hitched a ride to Cork from Cappoquin
the evening of the thirtieth of May.
The man that drove me was a traveling man
with some sort of a garment company
so there were ladies' garments in the back
in boxes with all sorts of literature,
but after a dozen words we hardly spoke,
except around a few jars at Lismore
where we met Mickey Keane who said the Duke
that had the local castle was his cousin
in a small way, only he'd had the luck
and Mickey hadn't was the only reason.
I honestly believed him but we went
before I could find out if this was true.
I figured you could make up what you want
about yourself in this country somehow,
having it your way—nobody really cared—
and where was there the harm to anyone,
particularly if he called himself a lord
like that one that belonged to Mickey Keane?
We were almost in Cork about this time.
I decided that my friend had had a bad
experience of some kind that kept him mum,
so I got out at the first stop I could,
wished him good luck and walked up Merchants Quay
toward Patrick Street, the thirtieth of May.

Michael Heffernan

THREE ANECDOTES

I

We made love in a field outside Gort
while the population was at mass.
You wanted to be caught by Christ himself
I guess, incinerated on the spot.
No one noticed. A cat
stared at a quivering leaf and wisps
of chimney smoke rose from the empty houses.
I discovered what nettles were when they
touched my thigh and stung. You laughed
at my surprise then drew me closer
while clouds moved in single-file from the sea
and assembled ahead. I stared abashed.
You said I'd learn to love this country.
Bordering tulips stammered and snapped.

II

We developed a yen for scaly fish
and bottom feeders. I learned to skin
still wriggling eels and soak the hard crust
off *fragach*. Plaice fought in my oven.
I slammed the door, dragged my line
on the sandy bottom again to snare
flounders unawares or perhaps a crab.
But what came up gave battle, a cuttle
spraying its camouflaging spit,
inky poison just missing my eye and once
in the boat its tentacles grabbed at my boot.
I watched its organs through transparent skin
turn purple, blue, then green, a bright bouquet
of dying taking, as always, much too long.

III

You found a younger girl for lover so turned
me into a woman overnight. Deep lines
appeared at my eyes and mouth, but that's just

79

"anecdotal," as the doctors say. Aging
was anyway overdue. By afternoon,
snow wiped out the road. Still I drove you
to the airport for your plane, navigating
the unbordered white by hearsay and respect
for what lay buried. Unaccountably
your laughter turned to dark hysteria.
I swerved. "Go on, we're late," you recomposed
yourself, lied and said you'd be all right.
Do we choose to leave as implausibly
as we choose to stay? Your face turned towards the gate.

Deborah Tall

80

TWO TRIPS TO IRELAND

1
Well-eye, gazing at daytime stars,
rain-speckle, patches of blooming mists,
a hillside white with water-spill,
a shower blowing inland at the coast...

All this water must *mean* something!

2
Long deserted glens in the Wicklow Hills
and an axe, buried in a tree so long
only the tip of the handle shows.

3
The small hotel in Gort, ale and roast lamb,
the midday drowse. Who breathed this air?
Who climbed these stairs? Time floats,
one face of a diamond, scraps of paper in the street.

4
From these ruined beehive huts
on the bright slope you can see
half the Dingle and
the distant winking sea.

Monks, who had to be
gone in the head.
Where's their god now?
Look closer at the cross-eyed pup
that followed you up this slant pasture,
the heifer that kneels, gazing out
on miles of sun and rain-washed air.

5
And the wind, a mind that's never still,
with its black thoughts, the rooks at Cashel,
its white thoughts, the sea gulls at New Grange,
all this tossing and cawing among great ruins.

6

Lissadell: cracks, tatters, stains.
An old lady in gumboots
shepherds a handful of tourists;
from an upstairs window
you strain to see the past,
horses like swans, peacocks on gravel,
cloudburst at four and dress for dinner...

Night fog. Ghosts in the garden,
ghosts on the stair,
ghost of an old fiddler, air threading the air.

7

On a back road by a tower
a movie crew, Arthurians lunching.
Why not? Time-levels mix like bones
in pasture-battlefield, bog-shrine.
Iseult still boils spuds for the pig
and Tristan, cutting turf, turns up
a Roman coin or a telephone cable.
That Viking ship below the Moher Cliffs
is a film prop or another fold
in the wrinkled suit of time.

8

The river Fergus
runs like a wild clock
by the tumbledown house we rent
on a cold lake in County Clare.
Near the ruins of the mill
I catch an eel and, feeling a fool,
I let him go.
A local rod and tackle man
who comes and goes like a ghost in the dusk
says I could have kept him 'for a pie,'
then hints at what I ought to know:
the trout are far too smart
to let themselves be caught
by a man so trapped in time.

David Young

82

CHRISTMAS IN DUBLIN

It is the cat within us—
roosting, eyes half-closed,
on the central heating vents
above the heart—
which holds us in Keegans'
where turkeys and ducks droop
from the ceiling.
It is this cat which wonders
at the power
that brings the speed
of these birds to zero.

While we buy cranberries,
leeks and lettuce
and joke about the gamey
smell nuzzling into our wools
and moulting hair, the cat
is rivetted to claws
tied to S-shaped hooks.
She sees the taut bodies
and bills pointing
like arrows through floorboards.
She knows the kill is not
complete until her teeth
touch the wishbone.

The cat
is calculating Christmas
dinner. This is the sparrows'
chance to possess the garden
and the juniper's fallen berries,
to dance on the window-ledge
in the peat fire's reflection
and to gather the guarded crumbs.

Nuala Archer

STAYING

Wherever night overtakes her—
that's where she stays.
Yesterday, night overtook her
waiting for a train.
She stayed on the platform.
Tonight she is watching
a candle burn an eye into the moon.
Night takes her over.
She stays at the typewriter
migrating through the blackened keys.

Nuala Archer

GREEN BEER

I

On Saint Paddy's Day, the jukebox plays
Bing Crosby singing "Galway Bay,"
And the color TV in this friendly dive
Is freckled with kilted dancers, live
Little dolls with their jigs and reels
Between the commercials for stomach pills.

The barman slides me another beer.
"On the house, Irish." "Good to be here."
He asks me—they all ask—what I think.
As always, I say the situation stinks.
"The murther and mayhem over there
Is somethin' a body can hardly bear,"
My brogue as phony as the beer is green.
The barman tops 'er up again.
The Gaelic lassies from the Bronx
Blur and fade as they end their dance.

II

In my drunken dream, a flag:
The Plough-stars in gold on a blue rag
Blurred by smoke. Kneeling beneath,
A shadow, on watch: an armed youth,
Fist clenched over the burning town.
Fading. Red sky. False dawn.
Then dead Cuchulainn bound to the tree,
The raven tearing at his eye.

James J. McAuley

i'm irish on the one side,
scottish on the other,
and my wallet was made in taiwan

as the sun sets on st. patrick's day,
i say to the kid behind the counter,

"before i decide how authentic i'm prepared to be
just exactly how much is your cheapest fifth of irish whiskey?"

he takes a look and says, "12.59."

"how much is your house-label bourbon?"

"4.11"

"it's a well-known fact," say i,
"that the irish are gifted
with astounding powers of make-believe.
wrap up the rotgut."

Gerald Locklin

THE VOICE OF AMERICA 1961

My hour switched on the cameras take.
The flash white of their advertisement roll:
beside the click faces in the colours
of the universe gaze upwards for my word.
I leave obscurity, stacking my symbols
on the shelf, Dollar, Steak, Mother (furies
of my springtime, a century and a half).
I was born in liberty and I cherish all,
so help me God, for the idealism of Lincoln,
Eisenhower, Kennedy, the kids on Main St.
At the cross bombs of history and ideology
I have prepared, the speeches typed,
and intercontinental missiles on alert;
the great heat presses: the buttons sweat.
I mount the stage to swear nuclear love,
for ever, even unto my ashes and dust.
The minute before I walk on I hesitate.
Between the wings with a book open on
his knees I catch sight of the old pioneer,
dove-eyed and his beard streaming in love.
Daddy Whitman, deployer of democracy,
serene in your chair of founder's timber,
let me steer close to touch YOUR BIG WHISKERS.

James Liddy

THE EMIGRANT IRISH

Like oil lamps we put them out the back,

of our houses, of our minds. We had lights
better than, newer than and then

a time came, this time and now
we need them. Their dread, makeshift example.

They would have thrived on our necessities.
What they survived we could not even live.
By their lights now it is time to
imagine how they stood there, what they stood with,
that their possessions may become our power.

Cardboard. Iron. Their hardships parcelled in them.
Patience. Fortitude. Long-suffering
in the bruise-coloured dusk of the New World.

And all the old songs. And nothing to lose.

Eavan Boland

WYNCOTE, PENNSYLVANIA: A GLOSS

A mocking-bird on a branch
outside the window, where I write,
gulps down a wet crimson berry,
shakes off a few bright drops
from his wing, and is gone
into a thundery sky.

Another storm coming.
Under that copper light
my papers seem luminous.
And over them I will take
ever more painstaking care.

Thomas Kinsella

LETTER FROM THE OLD SOD

Sandymount
Miltown Malbay
County Claire
Dec. 12, 1932

My Dear Brother:

It is now drawing near xmas
and time to write a few lines
to those that are far away
hoping to find ye all
in the very best of health
as this leaves everybody here
at present thank God.

Though I don't write often
I don't forget ye
father and Martin and wife are fine
also John and wife and family
but we don't see James
but very seldom.

Times are a bit hard nowadays
in every country as well as here.
The labourers are the best off
here now. For they have work
in the roads and quarries
and they get five shillings a day.
There is nothing for cattle
we couldn't even sell
one beast the fair day.

Mr. Connell he left us in a way
that we won't have a bite for anything.
I didn't need put anyone out
looking for him he landed here
August 16th just the same as a bailiff.
He was married and wanted to buy cattle.
But he did fix the house and bought an old cow.
Then the first of November
she was to be here.

But a week later he disappears
leaving the cow to Tim Hogan
to milk and take it home with him.

So he lands one night around 10 o'clock
having wife and luggage without
one spark of fire nor light
nor one to say God save you
or where did you come from.

She seems to be a nice woman alright.
I met her in church one morning
but I didn't go near them or invite them.
He used to tell some she was from Galway
another time from Mayo and now she's
from East Claire. She is Mrs. Connell
anyway but nobody knows her name.
He'd come and go just like the
Casey's and the Carthy's. But
I've said enough about him now.

Michael Hogan is home for the last few months.
his father was buried a month before he came.
I have no more to say now.
Father has just landed in with his walking stick.
Wishing ye all a very merry xmas.

                              your fond sister

Dennis Maloney

AT TRINITY COLLEGE

In Trinity's front square,
I rest companionless
beside the Campanile.
My gaze goes up to a blue-faced clock
which seems to say
it is half-past my life;
it goes down as if to search
for the years of my lost youth.
I wonder how I could have grown
            so old
without ever once holding hands
with a Celtic beauty
in the basement Buttery.

I have watched sex stalk this campus
in every shape and size,
petite girls pointedly
putting their best fronts forward,
bulge upon bulge beneath sweaters
of all sensual colors,
taller girls stretching trim legs forever.

I have coveted in secret
these products of eighteen or more
years of Irish milk and exercise,
dreaming of Deirdres, Mauves
and a Nuala I may never know.
But I am no *Ginger Man*—
my lust must not touch them.
My projected major is monogamy

Eugene Platt

the trees in their tropical headdress

the trees in their tropical headdress   & I in my
green satin jacket for jogging   that could be
mistaken   as racing silks   if there was a number
pinned to the back.   The Churchyard so green
the Hulk could have strolled there   completely
camouflaged   the cherry blossoms denting his hair.
All this green   it must be Ireland!   Come at last
to me!
    I thought the banner on the steeple said
     "Christ is Irish!"
instead of simply   "Christ is Risen"

Maureen Owen

93

Celebrations:
First Appearance Poems

OF, OR FROM

These sons
become me

having bent
me forward

at birth, back-
ward through life

these sons, these
boys become

me they take,
from the first,

the juices of me,
blood, love

my slickness they
become me

the notes of me
swallowed, they

eat what I sing,
these sons, they

become what
I wish, muscle

of me, spittal,
my luna

their hearts,
their night hearts

yaw, career
in my chest,

the black of them
me, and the shine

of them, them,
these sons they

become me they
become me.

Paul T. Hogan

fear of irish sons

—for my father's father

I have this notion of you: Irish,
dirt under haphazard fingernails,
a solid stride I suppose. Life,
work, one and the same, humor
at any fool's expense, especially
your own. The flashing hands
of a leprechaun.

There are no pictures. No
black and white snaps of you
curling up on black tagboard,
no comments from my mother, like:
"That's him when your father
was seven or so," or "There he is
outside the parish, in Cork—
or would it be Clare."

My father straddles between us,
silent about you. I guess
I think it makes some difference
that I am his first son
as he was yours. He has always
been silent about you.

I put age in his face. Ruts
that trace the grace of taking on
all comers: no questions, no
foolish twitch for answers.
I give him white hair, I stretch
his back and stoop him over,
trying to see you. I sit him down,
make him just bloody tired.
I fear for my first son.

Paul T. Hogan

my father, far in some hospital

I startle him with my late
long-distance call,
ringing him back
from his closed-eyed
remembering to the dimmed
sea-green or bone-white
hushed room.

"I'm holding
up fine...It isn't as bad..."
We squeeze the coiled
phone cord with our cool
free hands and he mumbles.
I push farther on, lightly
talk around it, around
his life, why

he still should rage for it.
Our half-opened eyes
roam the blank sheets
molded around him. "Yes,"
he gives in, almost unheard,

"a catheter..."
in through his groin
up the fat artery
into his wobbly heart.
"I'm too old," he tacks on
through the buzz in the line,
stopped, waiting

for me to say, "Yes,
skip the bypass. Five
or ten years at your
more or less age. Maybe
a diet, and stop moving."

Gently he breathes out
"Goodnight, love."
"Yes,"
      I rage gently,
"Goodnight."

Paul T. Hogan

two poems on sunday

—for my mother and her father

1. visit at one

My grandfather's bones
and nicotine skin half-step
through uncut spring lawn
back of Buff State Psychiatric,
moored against wind by his final
and first daughter's arm, muttering.
He smiles toothless and thin, his eyes
tint a bright green world
yellow, he watches me look
at my face in them, flashed back
to me yellow, and younger:

    At home on a snow-muffled night,
parents out, some time before
Buff State was home for him,
he stopped at our house for support,
bent to the wind and the yellowing
world, already lost, already lost, his
last spark of sense stunned
as I screamed with the force of a first
grandson's terror that I was not
to let him come in, that Mom told me
to send him back home
to wait to be called—he
shuffled away from the twice-locked
back door, struck dumb and blind

when he asks, the third time
this visit about school, I tell him
a joke, and his laugh makes us freeze:
while he coughs up his laugh, coughs
up his smile, coughs up his sense
like a sickness, his final
and first daughter's arm
half-steps him back.

2. seven-thirty pm

You call with your plan for my evening:
"We must talk," with a dark wash
of drama, "bring your brother, but wait
until after your father is gone."

You have notes on a pad as we enter,
to your left, a vague Chinese man
carved in the lamp looks them over,
grinning at something his painted eyes see.
You keep him close, like a husband.

Tonight, you soliloquize death
while we, your two taciturn sons
slide an ashtray back and forth
between us, aware mostly
you want us to break you

if age chips the edge of your senses,
or cracks split your patterns:
your life must shatter
with the drama of priceless bone china,
not face like some porcelain knick-knack
in the dust of a case
no one recalls.

Paul T. Hogan

A HOLY WELL

I'll drink if I can find it,
but in Ireland now
these springs are unattended,
their wallsteads fallen
into pasturage. Signs
that led me a quarter-mile
beyond the new suburb
leave me here, with the saint's
roofless church open as
a dory to the sky. Outside
and in, centuries of the dead,
mounds and depressions
the sheep are sexton to.
The farmer, almost as modern
as I am wears a face
passionless as a board
when I climb his wall by
a stair of jutting stones,
one eye out for his bullocks
and one for the minor
penance of their droppings.
Sourney, Boden, Gobnait—these
saints with small-town names
never walked on water. But
the mice trusted them,
and they knew which branch
to tap the ground with
so a spring bubbled up
to plump a child
from a rickle of bones.
Somewhere in this unmown grass
there may be a pagan water hole
that got christianized, where
I'll drink knowing brand names
haven't cured me, loving
the nerve of a common place
that's holy. If this one
isn't muffled in chloroplasm,
if there's a fish circling
its depths like a golden torque,

104

I'll drink to the miraculous
ordinary: a wren entrusting
an egg to a saint's hand.

Brendan Galvin

DONEGAL

Bog cotton and whin. A stone
gets up and is a black-faced
sheep. Between a fog
and a rain, mist hangs,
vaporous as the lace
across these *Gaeltacht* windows.

Now I understand
why treelessness and
bog that keeps brown water
are in me like a code,
Grandfather. These crossroads
where I try to place you
could be on Iceland
or the moon, and all
I hoard of you won't fill
the shallowest socket
rain has worked in limestone.

Were you to stand under
a signpost here, translating
An Clochan Liath for me,
I wouldn't know you
as I don't know what flowers
ascetically out of these rocks.
But as if the dead
merely exile themselves
to wander with the sheep,
I still expect you here,
maybe among the offspring
of some O'Donnell chief,
hiding out another century.

Which of these golden beaches
curving west toward Massachusetts
help you at the Cape
long after summer? What lough
do I render to your name;
which crossing of three roads
and red-haired children?

There was a Viking back there
in our turfpile, behind a child's
version of your face, and some
of us are redheads still.
But to say how the world began
where sheep lie down for
the journey into quartzite,
I will have to learn that single
jog of the head
men use to speak paragraphs
on the weather and the hard road
around here, where a lark
goes up each morning,
singing to penetrate the sun.

Brendan Galvin

INVENTING BALLYGALVIN

Because my cousin the priest
knows but won't tell me
where the family's from, I've invented
this West Cork townland. I admire
its sheepdogs' individual styles
as one has at my car head-on
and another snipes from wayside fuschia.

Both have a leg outstanding—
that "fender-duster" that heals
a different wrong way
on every dog. Still, as we say
in Ballygalvin, "He couldn't drive it
if he caught it, could he?"

All that walking topiary ahead
is only the backs of sheep.
For centuries now the castle's
been dropping in on their pasture,
a way of measuring time
stone by stone. When they get there
they'll gaze out bowmen's slots;
they like to pretend
they're the Norman invaders.
It's a kind of revenge,
though they're more like tumbleweeds
when wind leans them
against the stone bridge.

There's no pink hotel here
for golfing monsignors
in green hats, only this bog
of moor grass and black rush,
which lubbers onto the road
full of years of rain.
But not today, so I'll hold my hour
and admire how a soft morning
dissolves that blue mountain
seamed with walls, and the
switchback road that brought me.

Bless me, St. Finclan,
from your niche in the wall.
We're local boys without stone
or well to our names, and nobody
recalls your miracle.
Mine's that a cousin just gave me
a nod and almost sent me into
the left hand ditch full of axles.

He's filling pot holes
for the county board,
one of those foxy pip-sippers
whose pace migrated
to the Massachusetts
Department of Public Works.
Turns out in the States
he used to be a priest.

Turns out that faces in Ireland
are faces in Boston,
somebody's rotating
the living and dead. Or that's
his theory, not orthodox.
He says I'll have to watch
I don't meet myself rounding a corner,
or some red-haired woman, glorified
in maroon, who I promised once
I'd murder Cromwell for her.

Brendan Galvin

LINES FOR GARETH AND JANET DUNLEAVY

I exhort and invoke for you
the little stars over a small place,
the minora sidera writers of this place,
the silence of walkers in the wind of that place.
These are continued. Yes, Wallace Stevens,
our stars come from Ireland and make
doves of fame and trouble in the confined house
of writers. The westwardness of everything
like coffin ships on the horizon.
The music in the sails walks everything,
specially the wind as pen.
The history of Ireland is a script
done in the night of the big pen,
whether in sail dip or in the quiet oar tunes
of the curragh. The westwardness of
sauntering by the light of the heart:
the Galway of the terror of all musical sounds
from the Dublin of the reality of all
verbal tropes. Night of the pens,
verbal long knives never asleep
(the day I was born Ernest Roehm
died and became a movie star).
I was born in English-speaking shoals
and I try to aid the sorcery of that
language, that ashen 18th century woman
whose petticoats explode into English
near-eloquence. History lit few lamps
in modern Ireland and made a dark night.
That is why without looking up we begin with stars.
Minor stars, minor league, on the surface.
We are not known for spelling or dressing well
on any of our walks through battle-
ruined pastures. We do not rebuild,
we listen to your walking. It crunches
on something soft as the heart of doves.
The bones of battle men and women
sleeping in green vestments. By the light
of the grave lamp we'll dig them up.
Why as for weeping, our stars will do that for us.
They do it very well in the dark night.
The reeds in the wind make lament

but there blows a quieter music:
the whole country walking in a silence
that talks like a dried flower.
School and shoal of the coffin and cheap earth
flowers for entwining and winding.
The funeral march of the 18th century
tramping through the nineteen eighties.
Fame flames of the dead saunter out Byzantium.
Then everything clears. The stars become writers,
the writers become walkers who grow silent
as they vanish with knife and pen into
a well-dressed eternal night.

The pastures that thrive under a star-lit dome.
The poison clings to the pens, doves climb on the knives.
Moonlight moved to Brighton Pier but moving
westwards in flower, past the Hartford
Insurance Company buildings, not the fire and life
but the fire folk: real fairies who travel
by big wind of mouth and through ashes
deep lain in grass to exhort us to trouble in
life life in trouble. Brilliance is never being out of trouble,
and the stars have arrived.

(Written for the Hibernia-Irlande-Eire exhibition at the University
of Wisconsin-Milwaukee's Library)

James Liddy

RESPECT

Thady, sixty years out of Donegal,
propped, overflowing his tall barstool,
my father's pal, the last, hollering:

"Jim was a decent man, he prayed every night
for his family; I'm glad to met his son.
Sure, he took the drop, but never gave in."

(They shared a horsebox in a Brooklyn slum,
a boarding house run by rheumatic Mrs Averril,
who pitted her rosary against the Atom Bomb.)

"But your uncle was a right whoremaster,
riding black women." Monaghan's father
fusses in the background; "Keep the party clean—"

Just as it was about to become interesting!
Thady, an old motor man, reverses gears,
rewinding the thread of those solitary years

To recall a summer evening in Donegal,
how he won the raffle in the Parish Hall.
First prize, a kiss from the prettiest girl.

His eyes moisten, his voice thickens;
he lays aside his daily, *Journal American*,
"I can still picture her shy expression."

Among gasoline fumes, run-down brownstones,
Thady still holds on to his lucky number,
waiting stolidly on the platform beside her,

How when he kissed her, there was a cheer.
"The one time in my whole life." Thoughtfully,
Thady looks back down into his chilled beer.

"But I have always respected women.
So did your father." The stale odour
of lives broken down, next to nothing,

yet, on the litter, that stray offering.

John Montague

CITY OF CORK

A man is coughing outside our window over
O'Driscoll's Pub. It is late, the skies
thin to night's light, a young Irish policeman
blue in his tight uniform patrols these streets
that my grim ancestors knew as well as I know
my New Mexican deserts, our high air.

      —This pilgrimage, long postponed.
      I, the first of my family to return
      trace the sources of the blood.

here where the Celtic beats as strong as the waves
smashing Kerry's coast where we also lived and died.

Now rain hammers the winding rivers of Cork City
where the Irish need only look into a mirror to discover
another enemy, another in the long cycle of betrayal,
churches like Roman banks guarding the real power.

All these centuries, my kinsmen. I see your pinched faces
in these streets. Did you stay here in this shambling
1840's hotel when it was new, if anything is ever new
in Erin? My kinsmen, you too must have sung as angels
do, with eyes sad as the seas, walked these ruins
still haunted by the White Lady, the Holy Tree,
High Kings of Tara, their battlecries are still in the wind

in the sadness of old Cork where the grey sea crashes
and pale gulls stalk the sky, scream in alien tongues.

Their voices are loudest tonight, in this past come new
to my eyes. The sea's mockery. Deep eyes of the stars
as this Irish night rushes in upon me.

Keith Wilson

CONTRIBUTORS NOTES

Nuala Archer (1955-) Teaches at Oklahoma State, *Whale on the Line* (1981) another book due from Gallery Press.

John Berryman (1914-1972) The Pulitzer prize-winning *Dreamsongs* were completed in Dublin.

Wendell Berry (1934-) Kentucky farmer, poet, prophet and man-of-letters. His most recent collection of poems is *Sabbath* (1987) North Point.

Eavan Boland (1944-) Born in Dublin, has taught at Bowdoin. Her most recent book is *The Journey* (1987) Carcenet/Arlen House.

Kathy Calloway (1943-) *Heart of the Garfish* (1982) won the Agnes Lynch Sterret Poetry Prize, also the author of *Heart of the Bloodroot Flower* (1982).

Paul Carroll (1927-) Chicago-born and educated, editor-publisher, poet, teaches at University of Illinois-Chicago Circle; *Odes* (1968).

David Cintino (1947-) Teaches writing and modern Irish literature at Ohio University, *Last Rites* (1985) Swallow/Ohio Press.

Robert Creeley (1926-) Senior Black Mountain poet, Gray Chair at SUNYAB, his most recent book is *Memory Garden* (1985) New Directions.

Ann Darr (1920-) Iowa-educated, radio writer, as well as holder of a commercial pilot license; *Riding the Fireworks* (1981) Alice James Books.

Alan Duggan (1923-) Teaches at Sarah Lawrence, *Collected Poems* (1985) Ecco Press.

Robert Francis (1901-1987) Amherst, Mass (Fort Juniper), *Collected Poems* (1976) University of Massachusetts Press.

Tess Gallagher (1943-) Teaches at Syracuse University; *Amplitude: New and Selected Poems* (1988) Gray Wolf.

Brendan Galvin (1943-) Teaches at Central Connecticut State College; *Seals in the Inner Harbor* (1986) Carnegie Mellon.

Eamon Grennan (1941-) Dublin-born, Harvard-educated, teaches at Vassar, *Wildly for Days* (1983) and *What Light There Is* (1987) Gallery Press.

Vicki Hearne (1946-) "An animal trainer who reads Wittigenstein" teaches at Yale; *Adam's Task: Calling Animals by Name* (1986) Knopf.

Paul Hogan (1955-) Studied with Creeley and Logan at SUNYAB, coordinates Poets in the Schools for Just Buffalo Literary Center.

Robinson Jeffers (1887-1962) Travelled to Ireland with his wife Una in 1929, published a remarkable sequence *Descent to the Dead* in 1933.

Michael Heffernan (1943-) Teaches at University of Arkansas, *To the Wreakers of Havoc* (1984) University of Georgia.

Robert Kelly (1935-) Teaches at Bard College, see his "Erin Tantra America;" *Not This Island Music* (1987) Black Sparrow.

X.J. Kennedy (1929-) Teaches at Tufts, editor as well as witty poet, *Cross Ties* (1985) Georgia Press.

Galway Kinnell (1934-) Pulitzer-prize winner, teaches at NYU, *The Past* (1985) Houghton Mifflin.

Thomas Kinsella (1939-) Dublin-born, teaches at Temple; poet, editor, translator of *Tain* (1976), *An Duaniare* (1980), *New Oxford Anthology of Irish Poetry* (1986).

James Liddy (1935-) Irish-born and educated, teaches at the University of Wisconsin-Milwaukee; *Moon and Star Moments* (1982) At Swim.

John Logan (1923-1986) Iowa-born, educated; taught at SUNYAB till his retirement. *The Bridge of Change* (1981) BOA Editions.

Gerald Locklin (1941-) Born in Rochester, New York, teaches in California (Long Beach); *A Constituency of Dunces* (1968) Slip Stream Press.

Dennis Maloney (1951-) Graduate of Syracuse University, landscape architect, poet and publisher of White Pine Press.

James J. McAuley (1939-) Dublin-born (Conglowes graduate), teaches at Eastern Washington University; *Recital* (1983) Dolmen Press.

Eugene McCarthy (1916-) Senator from Minnesota, 1958-70 and candidate for president in 1968; *Ground Fog and Night* (1979).

John Montague (1929-) Brooklyn-born, Ireland's love poet, will be poet-in-residence at SUNY-Albany 1989; *Mount Eagle* forthcoming.

Marianne Moore (1887-1972) Legendary Brooklyn librarian and poet, *Complete Poems* (1981), *Complete Prose* (1985).

Joan Murray (1948-) Born in New York City, now lives in Rochester; *Egg Tooth* (1975), poems in *Hudson Review, Paris Review, APR.*

Maureen Owen (1943-) Minnesota-born; *Hearts in Space* (1980), *Zombie Notes* (1985).

Eugene Platt (1939-) South Carolina poet and activist, studied at TCD, now works with US Department of Labor, *South Carolina State Line* (1980).

Wallace Stevens (1879-1955) Pulitzer-prize winning poet and insurance executive, though he never travelled to Ireland, corresponded with Irish poet Thomas McGreevy.

James Schevill (1920-) Teaches at Brown University, *Ambiguous Dancers of Fame: Collected Poems, 1945-85* Swallow/Ohio Press (1987).

Nancy Sullivan (1929-) Teaches at Rhode Island College, *Body English* (1972).

Deborah Tall (1951-) Teaches at Hobart-William Smith, author of *The Island of the White Cow: Memories on an Irish Island* (1986) Atheneum.

Keith Wilson (1927-) Teaches at New Mexico State, his native state; *Lion's Gate: Selected Poems, 1963-1986* (1988) Cinco Puntos.

Terrence Winch (1945-) New York-born and educated at Fordham; musician and poet, *Irish Musicians/American Friends* (1985) Coffee House.

David Young (1936-) Educated at Yale, and a Shakespeare scholar as well as poet, teaches at Oberlin; *Earthshine* (1988) Wesleyan.

ACKNOWLEDGEMENTS

Nuala Archer, "Christmas in Dublin" and "Staying" from *Whale on the Line*. Dublin. Gallery Press, 1981. Reprinted by permission of the author.

Excerpts from *The Dreamsongs* by John Berryman. Reprinted by permission of Farrar, Straus and Giroux, Inc.

"To William Butler Yeats," Copyright © 1972 by Wendell Berry. Reprinted from his volume *The Country of Marriage* by permission of Harcourt Brace Jovanovich, Inc.

Evan Boland, "The Emigrant Irish," from *The Journey* Carcanet/Arlen House, 1987. Reprinted by permission of the author.

Kathy Callaway, "Love in the Western World," was published first in *The Nation*. Reprinted by permission of the author.

"Father," Copyright © Big Table Magazine and Paul Carroll. Reprinted by permission of the author.

"Parnell," from *Last Rites and Other Poems*, by David Cintino (Ohio State University Press, 1980) pp. 38-39. Reprinted by permission of the author.

"Theresa's Friends," from *Later* by Robert Creeley. Copyright © 1979 by Robert Creeley; used by permission of New Directions Publishing Corp.

Ann Darr "Gaelic Legacy" from *St. Ann's Gut*, Wm. Morrow & Co. Copyright © 1971 by Ann Darr; and "Looking for Origins" from *The Myth of a Woman's Fist*, Wm. Morrow & Co. Copyright © 1973 by Ann Darr. Reprinted by permission of the author.

"Mockery Against the Irish Censorship" and "On Being Out-Classed by Class" Copyright © 1961, 1962, 1968, 1972, 1973, 1974, 1983 by Alan Dugan from *New and Collected Poems, 1961-1983* by Alan Dugan. Published by The Ecco Press in 1983. Reprinted by permission.

"The Celt," "Ireland," and "Cromwell" reprinted from *Robert Francis: Collected Poems, 1936-1976* (Amherst: University of Massachusetts Press, 1976), Copyright © 1936, 1964, 1965, 1968 by Robert Francis.

"The Ballad of Ballymote," from *Under Stars*. Copyright © 1978 by Tess Gallagher. Reprinted by permission of Graywolf Press.

"Potso, My Wine-Dark Uncle" from *The Minutes No One Owns* (1977) "Just In Case You're Wondering Who You Are" from *Winter Oysters* (1983) "A Holy Well," "Donegal" and "Inventing Ballygalvin." Copyright © Brendan Galvin, reprinted and first printed by permission of the author.

"Anthropology," from *God's Mistress* (New York: Harper & Row, 1984), reprinted by permission of the author.

Eamon Grennan, "Gentle Art" and "Taking My Son to School." from *Wildly for Days* (Dublin, Gallery Press, 1983), reprinted by permission of the author.

"Soliloquy" reprinted from *Nervous Horses* by Vicki Hearne. Copyright © 1980 by the University of Texas Press. By permission of the author and the publisher.

"Of, or from," "fear of Irish sons," my father far in some hospital," two poems on Sunday," Copyright © Paul T. Hogan (1987), printed by permission of the author.

"Kennedy" by Michael Heffernan is reprinted by permission of the publisher from *The Cry of Oliver Hardy* by Michael Heffernan. Copyright © 1979, The University of Georgia Press. "Fathers," and "The Way West" by Michael Heffernan are reprinted by permission of the author from *To the Wreakers of Havoc* (University of Georgia Press.) Copyright © 1984 by Michael Heffernan.